STOP RUNNING AWAY

Ten Tips to Help You Bloom
Where You Are Planted

Mrs. Dion Lucas

Copyright © 2018 TEACH Services, Inc.

ISBN-13: 978-1-4796-0875-1 (Paperback)

ISBN-13: 978-1-4796-0884-3 (ePub)

TEACH Services, Inc.
PUBLISHING
www.TEACHServices.com • (800) 367-1844

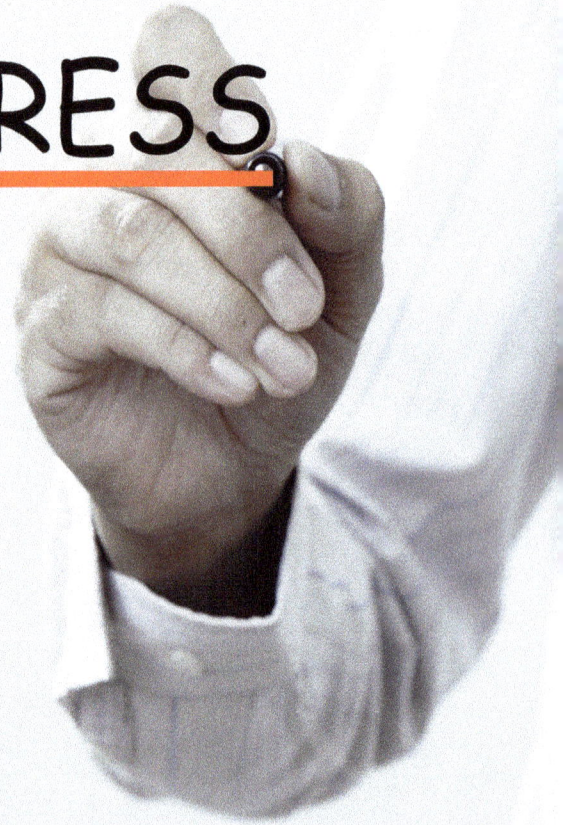

STOP RUNNING AWAY

Feeling overwhelmed? Feeling just a little grouchy? Everyone needs tools to cope with stress. Listed in this book are ten tips to balance that stress so that you can bloom where you've been planted. This resource is provided by the National Runaway Safe Line at www.1800RUNAWAY.org

1. TALK TO SOMEONE

Talk to someone you trust. A trusted person can be a friend, coworker, spouse, relative, pastor, counselor, or therapist. People who talk about their problems are usually happier and less stressed out.

2. EXERCISE

Exercise for a half hour three to five times a week. Medical studies have proven for centuries that physical fitness is a strong component to improving and maintaining a healthy lifestyle. Thirty minutes of walking throughout the day can improve mood, increase blood flow, and generate creative ideas.

3. MEDITATE

Try meditation. Listen to soft music as you close your eyes and breathe deeply. There's always comfort in knowing that no matter what path life takes you can make any situation work out for good with the right attitude and a good support system.

4. GET ENOUGH SLEEP

Try to get enough sleep every night. Wellness advisors encourage people to get between seven and nine hours of daily sleep. After a good night's rest, people can think clearly.

5. FIND A HOBBY

Identify something you like (sports, dancing, art, music...) and then do it! Find whatever you are passionate about and make time for it in your weekly or monthly activities. This passion of interest can play a huge part in your relationships with people.

6. EAT WELL

Eat well. A diet high in sugar or caffeine can increase stress and affect people's moods. Therefore, seek to eat a balanced diet consisting of fruits, vegetables, lean proteins, and good carbs.

7. RELAX

Spend time relaxing. Take a warm bath or shower, light a candle, and put on music. Renew yourself daily to get a fresh perspective and to be ready for tomorrow.

8. ENCOURAGE YOURSELF

Encourage yourself. When you feel good about who you are, you may not feel so stressed out. Uplift yourself with positive words and don't believe the negative lies.

9. PAY ATTENTION

Pay attention to what stresses you out. Can it be changed? Can you look at things differently and then feel less stressed about them? If you can't change it, then FLUSH IT! Let going to the restroom be your symbol of removing all the waste, drama, and burdens that life daily endeavors to shower upon you.

MENTAL HEALTH

GO

10. SEEK PROFESSIONAL HELP

Don't depend on recreational drugs and alcohol to help you. Recreational drugs, as well as the misuse of alcohol, can make your life problems more complicated. However, do follow doctors' advice when taking prescription drugs and don't be afraid to seek professional counseling.

TEACH Services, Inc.

P U B L I S H I N G

We invite you to view the complete
selection of titles we publish at:
www.TEACHServices.com

We encourage you to write us
with your thoughts about this,
or any other book we publish at:
info@TEACHServices.com

TEACH Services' titles may be purchased in
bulk quantities for educational, fund-raising,
business, or promotional use.
bulksales@TEACHServices.com

Finally, if you are interested in seeing
your own book in print, please contact us at:
publishing@TEACHServices.com

We are happy to review your manuscript at no charge.